SNAKES

ANACONDAS

James E. Gerholdt
ABDO & Daughters

Published by Abdo & Daughters, 4940 Viking Drive, Suite 622, Edina, Minnesota 55435.

Library bound edition distributed by Rockbottom Books, Pentagon Tower, P.O. Box 36036, Minneapolis, Minnesota 55435.

Printed in the United States.

Cover Photo credit: Photo Researchers, Inc.
Interior Photo credits: Peter Arnold, Inc. pages 11, 17, 19, 21
Photo Researchers, Inc. 5, 7, 9, 15

Edited by Julie Berg

Library of Congress Cataloging-in-Publication Data

Gerholdt, James E., 1943
    Anacondas / James E. Gerholdt.
    p. cm. — (Snakes)
Includes bibliographical references (p. 24) and index.
ISBN 1-56239-512-2
1. Anaconda—Juvenile literature. [1. Anaconda. 2. Snakes.] I. Title. II. Series:
Gerholdt, James E.,   1943- Snakes.
QL666.063G47   1995
597.96—dc20
                        95-18608
                        CIP
                        AC

About the Author

Jim Gerholdt has been studying reptiles and amphibians for more than 40 years. He has presented lectures and displays throughout the state of Minnesota for 9 years. He is a founding member of the Minnesota Herpetological Society and is active in conservation issues involving reptiles and amphibians in India and Aruba, as well as Minnesota.

Contents

ANACONDAS 4

SIZES 6

COLORS 8

WHERE THEY LIVE 10

WHERE THEY ARE FOUND 12

SENSES 14

DEFENSE 16

FOOD 18

BABIES 20

GLOSSARY 22

INDEX 23

BIBLIOGRAPHY 24

ANACONDAS

Anacondas belong to one of the 11 snake families. There are four anaconda **species**, two of which are rare. The green anaconda and the yellow anaconda are common.

A snake is a **reptile**, which is a vertebrate. This means they have a backbone, just like a human.

Anacondas are **cold blooded**. They get their body temperature from lying in the sun, on a warm log, or the warm ground. If they are too cool, their bodies won't work. If they get too hot, they will die. This is because their bodies need to be at a certain temperature.

Anacondas are also called water boas because they are often found in the water.

The green anaconda is a common snake.

SIZES

The green anaconda is the heaviest and probably the longest snake in the world. One anaconda killed and measured in Colombia was 37.5 feet (11.4 m) long. Some may be longer.

It is hard to measure a large anaconda. They are very strong. A 30-foot (9 m) snake would weigh several hundred pounds (136 kg).

The average length for a green anaconda is about 19 feet (5.8 m). The yellow anaconda is only six to seven feet (1.8 to 2.1 m) long.

*The anaconda is the heaviest and probably the longest
snake in the world.*

COLORS

The green anaconda is greenish in color with large, dark spots on the back. The snake's sides have smaller spots with light centers. As a green anaconda gets older, its color darkens.

The yellow anaconda is lighter in color than the green anaconda. The spots are smaller and more numerous. Both **species** have a spear-like marking on the top of the head.

Anacondas have colored spots on their back and sides.

WHERE THEY LIVE

Anacondas like water. They live in tropical river valleys, swamps, **marshes**, and other watery **habitats**.

Anacondas like slow-moving streams. They also like to sun themselves on branches that hang over the water. How far they wander from water is not known.

Anacondas like water. They live in tropical river valleys, swamps, and marshes.

WHERE THEY ARE FOUND

Anacondas are found along the Amazon River system in the northern half of South America. The green anaconda makes its home in Colombia, Venezuela, the Guianas, the island of Trinidad, Brazil, and Bolivia.

The yellow anaconda is found in Bolivia, Paraguay, Uruguay, Brazil, and Argentina. The other two **species** are found only on Marajo Island in Brazil.

VENEZUELA

GUYANA

SURINAME

FRENCH
GUIANA

COLOMBIA

Amazon River

*Marajo
Island*

ECUADOR

BRAZIL

PERU

BOLIVIA

PARAGUAY

CHILE

URUGUAY

ARGENTINA

Detail Area

*Anacondas are found
along the Amazon River
system in the northern
half of South America.*

13

SENSES

Anacondas and humans have four of the same senses. But anacondas have trouble seeing anything that isn't moving. Their **pupils** are **vertical**, which helps them to see better in the dark, when they are often active. These vertical pupils open in the dark to let in more light.

Like all snakes, anacondas have no ears and cannot hear. They feel vibrations through bones in the lower jaw.

Smell is their most important sense. All snakes use their tongue with which to smell. The tongue picks up scent particles and brings them back into the mouth. Without the tongue, an anaconda could not find its food.

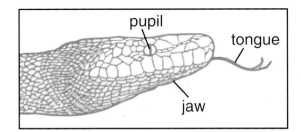

Anacondas have trouble seeing anything that isn't moving. Their pupils are vertical, which helps them to see better in the dark.

DEFENSE

Anacondas blend in with their surroundings. This is called **camouflage**. It is their most important defense against their enemies, which may be humans or large **predators** such as jaguars.

If an enemy can't see it, the snake is safe. If it senses danger, an anaconda will dive into the water and swim away. Or it may go to the bottom of a stream or lake. It won't surface until it is safe to come out again. The anaconda can hold its breath for a long time.

An anaconda also has a mouth full of sharp teeth. Even though there is no **venom**, the bite is painful!

An anaconda will dive into the water and swim away when it senses danger.

FOOD

A hungry anaconda will eat any animal it can swallow. It eats fish, birds, **mammals**, and **reptiles**.

The **capybara**, the world's largest **rodent**, is one of the anaconda's favorite meals. Any type of animal that lives near the water may also be eaten including **caiman**, a South American alligator.

Hidden by its **camouflage**, the anaconda catches its food by keeping still. When its **prey** comes along, the snake strikes out and grabs it. Then the snake **coils** around its prey and **suffocates** it. Once the animal is dead, the snake swallows it, usually head first.

This yellow anaconda is coiling around a caiman.

BABIES

Baby anacondas are born live. A female green anaconda can have 20 to 80 babies. The larger the female, the more babies she will have. The size of the babies depends on the size of the mother.

A newborn green anaconda is often two feet (61 cm) long. Like all snakes, the baby sheds its skin for the first time at the age of seven to ten days. This shedding is called **ecdysis**. As it grows, the snake continues to shed whenever its old skin gets too small.

A baby anaconda in a Venezuelan rainforest.

GLOSSARY

Caiman (KAY-man) - A large reptile of Central and South America, closely related to the alligator.

Camouflage (CAM-a-flaj) - The ability to blend in with the surroundings.

Capybara (kap-uh-BAR-uh) - A South American rodent with a coarse coat of brown, bristly hair.

Coil - To wind around and around into a pile.

Cold-blooded - Animals that get their body temperature from an outside source.

Ecdysis (ek-DIE-sis) - The process of shedding the old skin.

Habitat (HAB-uh-tat) - An area in which an animal lives.

Mammals (MAM-alls) - Warm-blooded animals with backbones that nurse their young.

Marsh - Low land at times covered by water.

Predator (PRED-uh-tor) - An animal that kills other animals for food.

Prey - An animal hunted for food.

Pupil (PEW-pill) - The opening in the eye's center where light enters.

Rainforest - A very thick forest in a place where rain is very heavy all through the year.

Reptile (REP-tile) - A scaly-skinned animal with a backbone.

Rodent - Any group of animals with large front teeth used for gnawing.

Species (SPEE-sees) - A kind or type.

Suffocate - To kill by stopping the breathing.

Venom (VEN-umm) - The poison of some animals.

Vertical (VERT-i-cull) - Up and down.

Index

A

alligator 18
Amazon River 12
Argentina 12

B

babies 20
backbone 4
birds 18
bite 16
Bolivia 12
bones 14
branches 10
Brazil 12

C

caiman 18
camouflage 16, 18
capybara 18
coil 18
cold blooded 4
color 8
Colombia 6, 12

D

defense 16

E

ears 14
ecdysis 20
enemies 16

F

family 4
fish 18
food 14, 18

G

green anaconda
    4, 6, 8, 12, 20
Guianas 12

H

habitats 10
head 8, 18
hearing 14
human 4, 14, 16

J

jaguar 16

L

lake 16
length 6
lower jaw 14

M

mammals 18
Marajo Island 12
markings 8
marshes 10
mouth 14, 16

P

Paraguay 12
predators 16
prey 18
pupil 14

R

reptile 4, 18
river valley 10
rodent 18

S

senses 14
shedding 20
size 6, 20
skin 20
smell 14
South America
    12, 18
species 4, 8, 12
streams 10, 16

strength 6
suffocation 18
swamps 10
swimming 16

T

teeth 16
tongue 14
trees 10
Trinidad 12

U

Uruguay 12

V

Venezuela 12
venom 16
vertebrate 4
vibrations 14

W

water 4, 10, 16, 18
water boa 4
weight 6

Y

yellow anaconda
    4, 6, 8, 12

BIBLIOGRAPHY

Mattison, Chris. *Snakes of the World*. Facts On File, Inc., 1986.

Mehrtens, John M. *Living Snakes of the World in Color*. Sterling Publishing Company, 1987.

Obst, Fritz Jurgen, Klaus Richter, and Udo Jacob. *The Completely Illustrated Atlas of Reptiles and Amphibians for the Terrarium*. T.F.H. Publications, Inc., 1988.

Peters, James A. and Braulio Orejas-Miranda, Catalogue of the Neotropical Squamata: Part 1. *Snakes*. Smithsonian Institution, 1970.

Pope, Clifford H. *The Giant Snakes*. Alfred A. Knopf, 1965.